THE SCIENCE BEHIND GYMNASTICS

by L. E. Carmichael

Consultant:

Mark Walsh
Associate Professor of Exercise Science
Miami University
Oxford, OH

CAPSTONE PRESS
a capstone imprint

Edge Books are published by Capstone Press,
1710 Roe Crest Drive, North Mankato, Minnesota 56003
www.mycapstone.com

Copyright © 2016 by Capstone Press, a Capstone imprint. All rights reserved. No part of this publication may be reproduced in whole or in part, or stored in a retrieval system, or transmitted in any form or by any means, electronic, mechanical, photocopying, recording, or otherwise, without written permission of the publisher.

Library of Congress Cataloging-in-Publication Data
Cataloging-in-publication information is on file with the Library of Congress.

ISBN 978-1-4914-8159-2 (library binding)
ISBN 978-1-4914-8163-9 (paperback)
ISBN 978-1-4914-8167-7 (ebook pdf)

Editorial Credits
Arnold Ringstad, editor
Craig Hinton, designer and production specialist

Photo Credits
Alamy: PCN Photography, 28, Stephen Barnes/Northern Ireland News Archives, 8; AP Images: 4, Charles Krupa, 12–13, EMPICS Sport/Press Association, 18, Julie Jacobson, 14 (right), 21, 24, Kyodo, 17, Matt Dunham, 16; iStockphoto: albertogagna, 10 (bottom), A-Digit, 14 (left); Red Line Editorial, 10–11, 28–29; Shutterstock Images: aliisik, 20, Andrey Kuzmin, 11 (bottom), Aspen Photo, 23 (top), Coprid, 11 (right), Dani Vincek, 11 (left), kayannl, 6–7, 26–27, Kellie L. Folkerts, 10 (top), Nicholas Rjabow, 22, Robyn Mackenzie, 11 (top), Sergey Golotvin, 1, 23 (bottom); Thinkstock: Dorling Kindersley, 6 (top), 6 (middle left), 6 (middle right), 6 (bottom), 7 (top), 7 (bottom), Ryan McVay/Valueline, cover

TABLE OF CONTENTS

Nadia Comaneci's performance in the 1976 Montreal Olympics earned her a place in gymnastics history.

THE HISTORY OF
OLYMPIC GYMNASTICS

Germany, 1800s
Friedrich Ludwig Jahn designs modern gymnastics equipment.

Athens, Greece, 1896
Men's gymnastics is one of seven sports in the first modern Olympic Games.

USA, 1930s
Gymnasts, divers, and skiers train on a new invention, the trampoline.

Munich, Germany, 1972
More people watch gymnastics than any other Olympic event.

Ancient Greece
Soldiers use gymnastics to train for battle.

Sweden, 1881
The International Gymnastics Federation (FIG) is founded.

USSR, 1920s
Rhythmic gymnastics becomes a sport.

Helsinki, Finland, 1952
The Olympic Games introduce individual gymnastics events for women.

CHAPTER 1

FASTER, HIGHER, **STRONGER**

It is July 18, 1976. The gymnastics event at the Montreal Olympics in Canada is underway. Fourteen-year-old Nadia Comaneci of Romania grips the uneven bars and starts her routine. Quick, precise, and powerful, she flows around the bars as lightly as a breeze. With a final twist and flip, she sticks her landing and waits for her score. A number flashes on the scoreboard: 1.00.

No one, not even Nadia, knows what it means. Then the announcer explains that the scoreboard can only show three digits. Nadia has scored a perfect 10.00.

The crowd goes wild! No female Olympic gymnast had ever earned a 10 before. But Nadia is not finished. She scores seven perfect 10s in Montreal, winning three gold medals, a silver, and a bronze. The gymnast becomes a legend.

Sydney, Australia, 2000
Trampolining becomes an Olympic sport.

Los Angeles, California, 1984
The Olympic Games introduce rhythmic gymnastics.

GYMNASTICS
APPARATUSES

Artistic gymnasts perform **skills** on different **apparatuses**. Men compete on the horizontal bar, the parallel bars, the rings, and the pommel horse. Women compete on the balance beam and the uneven bars. Both men and women compete on the vault and the floor exercises.

Horizontal Bar
» 94.5 inches (240 centimeters) long
» 110.2 inches (280 cm) from floor

MEN'S

Parallel Bars
» 137 inches (348 cm) long
» 78.7 inches (200 cm) above floor
» 16.5-20.5 inches (42-52 cm) between bars

Rings
» 110.2 inches (280 cm) above floor
» 19.7 inches (50 cm) apart
» diameter of each ring: 7.1 inches (18 cm)

Pommel Horse
» 63 inches (160 cm) long
» 13.8 inches (35 cm) wide
» upper surface 45.3 inches (115 cm) from floor
» pommels (handles) 15.8-17.7 inches (40-45 cm) apart

skill—a gymnastics move such as a cartwheel, somersault, or swing
apparatus—equipment that gymnasts use in artistic gymnastics routines

Then and Now

Nadia competed in artistic gymnastics. This involves short routines using a variety of apparatuses. Artistic gymnastics was the only type included in the 1976 Games. Today women can also compete in the rhythmic gymnastics event. They perform floor routines with ribbons, hoops, ropes, clubs, or balls. Men and women both take part in a separate event called trampolining.

Whether a gymnast is swinging, somersaulting, or gripping a pommel horse, scientific principles are at work. From physics to nutrition to **psychology**, the athletes who go for the gold must learn and master the science behind gymnastics.

Balance Beam
» 196.9 inches (500 cm) long
» 4 inches (10 cm) wide
» 49.2 inches (125 cm) from floor

Uneven Bars
» 94.5 inches (240 cm) long
» upper bar 98.4 inches (250 cm) from floor
» lower bar 66.9 inches (170 cm) from floor

WOMEN'S

Olympic gymnasts must train hard to build up their strength.

Early Training

Olympic gymnasts usually start training when they are five or six years old. Their training changes as they grow. If you want to be an Olympic gymnast, it is important to start training early. Most gymnasts need eight to 12 years of practice before their bodies—and minds—are ready for the Olympics.

CHAPTER 2

BUILDING A GYMNAST'S BODY

Before they go for gold, gymnasts must learn dozens of complicated skills. Trainers help gymnasts prepare physically using knowledge of human physiology. To perform safely, they must first build muscle strength and **flexibility**.

Gymnasts build strength by lifting weights. Weight lifting tears muscle fibers. The fibers then grow back thicker and stronger. This helps muscles grow. Strength is most important in events such as the rings, where gymnasts hold their bodies steady against the downward force of **gravity**. Other events, such as the vault, require explosive muscle power. Gymnasts in these events need to push with a lot of force at once. They need muscles that work well in quick, powerful movements. Lifting very heavy weights can help build these fast muscle fibers.

flexibility—the ability to perform a movement through a large range of motion

gravity—a force that causes objects to move toward Earth's center

FEEDING A GYMNAST

Food gives gymnasts energy for training and growth. A healthy diet also helps prevent injuries. Calories, especially those from protein, let gymnasts put on weight and muscle mass. This helps them get stronger.

Carbohydrates

Purpose: main source of energy

Average 10-year-old needs: 7.9 ounces (225 grams) daily

Training gymnast needs: 13.1 ounces (372 g) daily

Gymnasts increase their flexibility by stretching. This increases the range of motion of an athlete's joints, which can decrease the risk of injuries. One stretch is the forward splits. During splits, the left and right legs separate and form a straight line. For many people, the very idea of this hurts! But gymnasts can do advanced stretches easily. They especially need flexibility for poses in rhythmic gymnastics.

Fat

Purpose:
energy, protecting organs

Average 10-year-old needs:
1.2 ounces (33 g) daily

Training gymnast needs:
2.1 ounces (59 g) daily

Vitamins and Minerals

Purpose: strong bones, carrying oxygen in the blood

Protein

Purpose: builds and repairs muscles

Average 10-year-old needs:
2.6 ounces (75 g) daily

Training gymnast needs:
3.4 ounces (96 g) daily

Fluid

Purpose: replaces sweat

Average 10-year-old needs:
8 cups (1.9 liters) daily

Training gymnast needs:
10–12 cups (2.4–2.8 L) daily

Shakin' All Over

Small differences in flexibility might make the difference between Olympic gold and silver. In 2006 scientists found a new way to help gymnasts get more flexible.

When practicing splits, gymnasts rested one leg on a special shaking box. One month later, they had improved their flexibility dramatically. Scientists think shaking may warm the muscles or help them relax during a stretch. Some teams, including the U.S. Olympic gymnasts, now use a shaking box when doing various stretches.

BRAIN TRAINING

Winning athletes train their brains as well as their bodies. Psychology helps gymnasts:

☑ **REDUCE STRESS:** Athletes attempt to respond to stress with excitement for their performance, rather than letting it have a negative impact on their routines.

☑ **CONTROL FEAR:** Some athletes listen to music right up until their performance, distracting them from fear about the competition.

☑ **SET GOALS:** Goals can help gymnasts focus their attention, improve self-confidence, and lessen their anxiety.

☑ **INCREASE THEIR CONFIDENCE:** Remembering successful routines that happened in practice can help gymnasts become more confident in their abilities during a big competition.

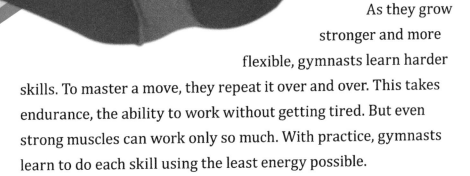

Olympic-level gymnasts are extremely flexible.

As they grow stronger and more flexible, gymnasts learn harder skills. To master a move, they repeat it over and over. This takes endurance, the ability to work without getting tired. But even strong muscles can work only so much. With practice, gymnasts learn to do each skill using the least energy possible.

Gymnasts take advantage of spring forces to launch themselves high into the air from the trampoline.

BOUNCE: THE PHYSICS OF
THE TRAMPOLINE

A

Downward force from muscles

B

Upward force from springs returning to original state

CHAPTER 3

UP, UP, AND AWAY:
TAKING OFF

Jumping. **Tumbling**. **Dismounts**. In every gymnastics event, athletes spend part of their routine soaring through the air. But before they can fly, they have to take off. A good takeoff depends on physics, the science of forces and motion.

Famous physicist Sir Isaac Newton developed three laws of motion in the late 1600s. His third law says that for every action, there is an equal and opposite reaction. The trampoline presents a great example of this law. When a gymnast jumps, her muscles push her feet against the trampoline bed. This downward force stretches the springs that connect the bed to the frame. Like elastic bands, the springs snap back into their original shape. This pulls the bed back up. The upward force has the same strength as the downward force of the gymnast's jump. It launches her into the air. By adding muscle force with every jump, the gymnast flies up to 30 feet (10 meters) high. That is plenty of room for twists and flips!

tumble—to spin or fly during a floor routine
dismount—to let go of or jump off an apparatus to finish a routine

Gymnasts launch themselves into the air from the vault using their arm muscles.

Too Much Friction

When swinging around a bar, the gymnast's hands slide over the bar's surface. This creates **friction**, which resists the motion of the hands. Friction causes the top layers of skin to separate from the deeper layers. This forms blisters. Strong friction can peel the skin right off. Gymnasts wear glovelike devices called grips to prevent blisters.

Gymnasts also use **elastic forces** when taking off during vault. To fly upward, gymnasts bounce on the springboard. Then they push against the vaulting table with their hands. Vault is different than trampoline. Gymnasts must fly horizontally as well as upward. To build horizontal speed, gymnasts run toward the table as fast as they can. They hit the springboard going as fast as 17 miles (27 kilometers) per hour.

friction—a force generated when objects slide past each other
elastic force—a force caused when an object, such as a spring, stretches or compresses

Takeoffs from the trampoline cause gymnasts to fly in straight lines. Gymnasts also fly straight when dismounting from the rings or bars. How can that be, when they start their takeoffs by swinging in circles? When the athlete lets go of the apparatus, some of the **angular momentum** instantly becomes **linear** motion. He flies straight in the direction he was traveling when he let go. Gravity then pulls him down, causing him to travel in an arc. Gymnasts time their takeoffs carefully to make sure they will go in the right direction.

This image shows the flight path of Japan's Kohei Uchimura during his vault performance in the 2012 London Olympics. Flight path is the distance and direction a gymnast travels through the air. It is a mixture of vertical and horizontal motion.

angular momentum—a measure of an object's rotation, involving mass, shape, and speed
linear—straight

German gymnast Anna Dogonadze tucks and spins during the trampoline competition in the 2012 London Olympics.

CHAPTER 4

TWIST, BEND, FLIP:
THE PHYSICS OF FLIGHT

Gymnastics is all about spinning. One way to make an object spin is by pushing on one end of it. This applies a twisting force called **torque** that causes rotation. During takeoff, the floor, trampoline, or apparatus pushes on the gymnast's hands or feet. That push creates angular momentum.

A gymnast cannot change her angular momentum while she's in the air. But like a falling cat, she uses muscle force to change her body's shape. She can somersault, twist, and spin to land on her feet.

Angular momentum makes a gymnast's body spin around an invisible line. This line is called the **axis of rotation**. It is a lot like the post in the center of a revolving door. The gymnast's arms and legs are like the door panels. The person's weight balances around his or her body's **center of mass**.

torque—force multiplied by the distance of the force from an object's center of mass
axis of rotation—the invisible line a gymnast spins around when doing a skill
center of mass—the place all weight in the body balances around

The amount of angular momentum depends on the amount of torque. The amount of torque depends on the placement of the force.

A B C

No torque.
No spin.
No angular momentum.

Small torque.
Slow spin.
Low angular momentum.

Large torque.
Fast spin.
High angular momentum.

When standing straight with her arms at her sides, the average gymnast's center of mass is behind her belly button. It is slightly higher for male gymnasts. If she lifts her right arm above her head and to the right, her center of mass moves too. It shifts up and to the right. Her axis of rotation runs through her center of mass. Shifting the center causes the axis to tilt. This tilt changes a somersault into a twist.

Body shape also affects how fast the gymnast spins. Bodies have **inertia**. They resist changes in speed and direction. Body parts that are farthest from the axis of rotation have the most inertia. To increase rotation speed, a gymnast reduces her inertia. She does this by making her body more compact. She pulls her arms into her chest or folds her straight body into a pike or tuck. A gymnast who does a double somersault in the pike position can add an extra spin by doing a tuck instead. That might be all it takes to go from a silver medal to a gold.

A)

When the gymnast is swinging, his axis of rotation runs along the bar.

AXIS OF ROTATION

inertia—a body's tendency to remain still or to continue moving at the same speed in the same direction

C)

When a gymnast twists in the air, her axis of rotation runs from her head to her feet.

B)

During a somersault, the gymnast's feet fly over her head. Somersaults can be forward or backward. The axis of rotation runs through her center of mass, which is just outside her body.

US gymnast Sam Mikulak sticks the landing after a vault performance in the 2012 London Olympics.

CHAPTER 5

STICKING IT:
SAFE LANDINGS

Even as a gymnast soars upward, gravity begins pulling him down. After a frozen moment at the top of his flight, he **accelerates** back toward Earth. His speed changes by approximately 32 feet (9.8 m) per second for every second in the air.

Force is mass multiplied by acceleration. On landing, a gymnast's speed quickly changes to zero. This fast acceleration can create a force of more than 14 times his weight. The force travels down into the landing mat. The mat resists with an equal and opposite force. To stick a landing, the gymnast controls this force with his muscles. The padding on the mat spreads this opposite force out over a longer time. It makes the landing softer.

accelerate—to change in speed or direction

COMING IN FOR A LANDING

Every flight is different, and so is every landing. To prepare for landing, a gymnast must:

1.
Move his legs into a position in which they will not be harmed during landing.

2.
Look for the landing mat.

Then, his brain and body take over:

3.
Using information from his eyes, his brain measures speed and time until landing.

4.

About 150 to 170 milliseconds before landing, his muscles tighten, protecting his body.

5.

To keep his balance after touchdown, he lifts or circles his arms.

Every landing has two stages. First, the part of the foot that initially touches down creates a small force. Second, a larger force comes when the whole foot hits the mat. Gymnasts soften a landing by increasing its duration. Toe-first landings take more time than heel-first landings. They spread out the force of landing over a longer period. That means toe-first landings feel softer, because they apply the force over a longer time. Gymnasts can also lengthen the landing time by letting their ankles and knees bend. During a soft landing, a gymnast's knees bend by more than 60 degrees.

Mats absorb force and increase landing time.

No More Perfect Ten

Once, artistic gymnasts dreamed of scoring a perfect 10. But in 2008 the International Federation of Gymnastics (FIG) launched a new scoring system. Their goal was to encourage gymnasts to aim "faster, higher, stronger," in keeping with the spirit of the Olympic Games.

Today, a gymnast receives two scores. One adds points for the difficulty of each skill in the routine. The other starts at 10 points, going down with every mistake. The two scores get added together. During the 2012 Olympics, gold-medal scores ranged from 15.191 to 16.533. There is no longer a clearly defined perfect score.

Landing force normally travels straight down through the mat and straight up through the gymnast's body. But if the gymnast is still twisting when he lands, the force twists as well. This can lead to knee, ankle, and back injuries. Slipping can also cause injuries. Friction from the cover of the landing mat helps prevent slips. Perfect landings are the finishing touch on dazzling routines, but they are very hard to do.

The ways gymnasts spring into the air, twist and flip in flight, and stick perfect landings are all dictated by the laws of physics. Psychology and nutrition play important roles in gymnasts' training. Top athletes must learn and master all these aspects of science to take home a medal.

Cover layer:
vinyl or carpeted surface provides friction to prevent slips

LANDING MATS

Top layer:
squishes under force so the landing feels soft

Middle layer:
stiff to support a gymnast's feet

Bottom layer:
thick and soft to decrease force and prevent injury

GLOSSARY

accelerate (ak-sel-uh-RAYT)—to change in speed or direction

angular momentum (ANG-gyu-lur mom-MEN-tuhm)—a measure of an object's rotation, involving mass, shape, and speed

apparatus (ap-uh-RAT-us)—equipment that gymnasts use in artistic gymnastics routines

axis of rotation (AK-siss UHV roh-TAY-shun)—the invisible line a gymnast spins around when doing a skill

center of mass (SEN-tur UHV MASS)—the place all weight in the body balances around

dismount (diss-MOUNT)—to let go of or jump off an apparatus to finish a routine

elastic force (i-LASS-tik FORSS)—a force caused when an object, such as a spring, stretches or compresses

flexibility (flek-suh-BIHL-uh-tee)—the ability to perform a movement through a large range of motion

friction (FRIK-shuhn)—a force generated when objects slide past each other

gravity (GRAV-uh-tee)—a force that causes objects to move toward Earth's center

inertia (in-UR-shuh)—a body's tendency to remain still or to continue moving at the same speed in the same direction

linear (LIN-ee-ur)—straight

psychology (sy-CALL-uh-gee)—the study of the mind

skill (SKIL)—a gymnastics move such as a cartwheel, somersault, or giant swing

torque (TORK)—force multiplied by the distance of the force from an object's center of mass

tumble (TUHM-buhl)—to spin or fly during a floor routine

READ MORE

Kawa, Katie. *The Science of Gymnastics.* Sports Science. New York: PowerKids Press, 2016.

Schlegel, Elfi, and Claire Dunn. *The Gymnastics Book: The Young Performer's Guide to Gymnastics.* Buffalo, N.Y.: Firefly Books, 2012.

Schwartz, Heather E. *Gymnastics.* Science Behind Sports. Farmington Hills, Mich.: Lucent Books, 2011.

CRITICAL THINKING USING THE COMMON CORE

1. Look at pages 6 and 7. Which apparatuses might allow gymnasts to fly highest into the air? What effect would this height have on the force of their landings? (Craft and Structure)

2. What do pages 10 and 11 tell you about nutrition for gymnasts? How might the purpose of each item come into play for a training gymnast? Support your answer with at least two other print or online sources. (Integration of Knowledge and Ideas)

INTERNET SITES

FactHound offers a safe, fun way to find Internet sites related to this book. All of the sites on FactHound have been researched by our staff.

Visit www.facthound.com

Type in this code: 9781491481592

Check out projects, games and lots more at
www.capstonekids.com

INDEX